one
mandala
a week

elizabeth jordan

One Mandala a Week
By Elizabeth Jordan
elizabethjordan@shaw.ca

Copyright ©2016 Elizabeth Jordan

ISBN: 978-1535559935

www.ingramcontent.com/pod-product-compliance
Lightning Source LLC
Chambersburg PA
CBHW052003280526
45793CB00005B/829